STRATHERN, PAUL
WITTGENSTEIN IN 90 MINUTES
3/1999

192
S

WITTGENSTEIN IN 90 MINUTES

Wittgenstein

IN 90 MINUTES

Paul Strathern

IVAN R. DEE
CHICAGO

Library of Congress Cataloging-in-Publication Data:
Strathern, Paul, 1940–
    Wittgenstein in 90 minutes / Paul Strathern.
      p.   cm. — (Philosophers in 90 minutes)
    Includes bibliographical references and index.
    ISBN 1-56663-130-0 (cloth : alk. paper). —
    ISBN 1-56663-131-9 (paper : alk. paper)
    1. Wittgenstein, Ludwig, 1889–1951.   I. Title.   II. Series.
B3376.W564S877   1996
192—dc20   96-24945

Contents

WITTGENSTEIN IN 90 MINUTES

Introduction

If we accept Wittgenstein's word for it, he is the last philosopher. In his view, philosophy in the traditional sense—as it had been known in the twenty-five centuries since it was started by the ancient Greeks—was finished. After what he had done to philosophy, it was no longer possible.

It is fitting that philosophy should end with its most limited practitioner. Ludwig Wittgenstein was a superb logician, and his solution to the problems of philosophy was to reduce them to logic. All else—metaphysics, aesthetics, ethics, finally even philosophy itself—was excluded. Wittgenstein sought the "final solution" for philosophy, with the aim of putting an end to it once and for all. He had one go at this, but it didn't work; so he had a second try that did.

Wittgenstein's Life and Works

Apart perhaps from Leibniz, Wittgenstein is the only major philosopher to have produced two distinct philosophies. And when one considers that both of these were dedicated to finishing off philosophy, one begins to get a measure of the man's perverse dedication.

His father had something to do with this. It is appropriate that Wittgenstein grew up just across town from where Sigmund Freud had recently installed the world's most famous couch. Wittgenstein's father Karl was a tyrant. By the time young Ludwig arrived on the scene his father was one of the uncrowned industrial kings of Europe (more powerful even than Krupp) and a predominant influence on the Viennese cultural scene (Brahms would play at home after dinner, and in the art world he personally funded the Vienna Sezession). Karl Wittgenstein had a domineering personality, a first-class intellect, a deep understanding of culture, and the self-assurance that he could charm the birds from the trees (on the days when he didn't feel like blasting them off the branches).

Karl's influence on his family was catastrophic. Young Ludwig had four older brothers, most of whom appear to have been brilliant, exceptionally highly strung, and homosexual. Three of them were to commit suicide, a possibility that Ludwig clung to like a talisman throughout his life. The other brother who survived became a concert pianist, had his right hand blown off in World War I, and afterward continued with his career, commissioning piano concertos for the left hand, including the celebrated one by Ravel. He was not considered to have been as brilliant as his other brothers, or even the best pianist.

Ludwig Wittgenstein was born April 26,

1889, and brought up in a palace on the exclusive Alleegasse (now called Argentinierstrasse) in Vienna. Although Wittgenstein was predominantly Jewish by blood, his family had become Christians, and he was baptized a Roman Catholic. He was educated by private tutors amidst an atmosphere of extreme cultural intensity (suicidal genius brothers practiced at the grand piano long into the early hours; a sister commissioned her portrait by Klimt and rejected the Goyas from the family collection because "their tone was out of place"). At the age of ten, young Ludwig single-handedly designed and constructed out of pieces of wood and wire a model sewing machine. By the time he was fourteen he could whistle entire movements from a number of well-known symphonies. These activities would seem to be the nearest he came to playing in the manner of an ordinary child.

In 1903 Wittgenstein left home for the first time to attend the Realschule in Linz, where he studied mathematics and science. Curiously, Hitler was at this school at the same time. They were both the same age and should have studied in the same class. Wittgenstein considered that he was a mediocre student, but he was nonetheless promoted to the year above his age group; Hitler records how he shone among his doltish classmates, but according to the records he was kept back in the year lower than his age group. So the whistling dolt and the supreme genius never met.

After this Wittgenstein studied mechanical engineering for two years at the Technische Hochschule at Charlottenburg in Berlin; and in 1908 he left to continue his studies in England. For the next three years he did research in aeronautics at Manchester University, and conducted experiments with kites at the Upper Atmosphere Station near Glossop in Derbyshire. At this stage he showed no sign of what was to come. He knew nothing about philosophy, and was considered by his colleagues quite bright though certainly not brilliant. In the typical English manner of the period, Wittgenstein's colleagues tended to regard him merely as an eccentric German. They were wrong: he was an eccentric Austrian—a rare but altogether more idiosyncratic breed.

Wittgenstein was punctiliously well-mannered yet capable of flying into a storming rage when anything went wrong with his experiments. In his relations with others he conveyed a cosmopolitan Viennese polish, but it soon became apparent to his colleagues that he hadn't the first idea of how to get along socially with ordinary people (which included anyone he was not likely to encounter among the geniuses, magnates, and government ministers who frequented the Wittgenstein household). He would work fanatically all day without a single break, then lie in a scalding bath all evening contemplating suicide. One Sunday when he and a colleague missed the train to Blackpool, Wittgenstein suggested they hire one for the two of them.

As part of his research, Wittgenstein set about designing a propeller. The problems posed by this led him into mathematical theory, which appears to have triggered in him some unconscious impulse. Within a remarkably short time his intellect focused, assuming all the power of his intense personality. The propeller and its attendant mathematics were soon forgotten as he continued questioning ever more deeply, until he was probing the very foundations of mathematics. It was as if his mind had locked onto the need to discover some utter bedrock of certainty in the world. It is perhaps no accident that around this time his brothers began comitting suicide and his father became ill with cancer.

Who knew about the foundations of mathematics? Wittgenstein was told of the recent pioneering work done by Bertrand Russell, and immediately he began reading Russell's *Principles of Mathematics*, the very latest work on the subject. In this, Russell set out to prove that the fundamentals of mathematics were in fact logical, and that all pure mathematics could be derived from a few basic logical principles. But Russell's attempt foundered on a paradox. Russell attempted to define numbers by using classes. Some classes are members of themselves, and some are not. For example, the class of human beings is not a member of itself because it is not a human being. The class of nonhuman beings, however, is a member of itself. But is the class of "all classes which are not members of

14

themselves" a member of itself? If it is, it is not. Yet if it is not, it is. The entire status of mathematics hung on this seemingly trivial paradox, which according to Russell affected "the very foundations of reasoning." He ended his book by issuing a challenge to "all students of logic" to solve it. Wittgenstein immediately launched into the fray. He emerged with a radical solution, dismissing the entire concept of classes as an unwarranted assumption.

Russell in his turn dismissed Wittgenstein's solution while at the same time admiring its ingenuity. But Wittgenstein was not so easily put off. In 1911 he traveled to Cambridge to see Russell, and there he decided to study philosophy with Russell and abandon engineering, the profession his father had chosen for him.

Russell had taken on a lot more than he'd bargained for. At the time he was arguably the leading philosopher in Europe; Wittgenstein had hardly read a book on the subject. Yet Wittgenstein took to turning up at Russell's rooms at all times of day and night, insisting upon engaging him for hours on end in the most intense "philosophical" speculations—sometimes to do with logic, sometimes to do with suicide. According to Russell, Wittgenstein had "passion and vehemence" and a feeling that "one must understand or die." Yet when he was convinced that he did understand, nothing would persuade him to the contrary. He refused to accept Russell's belief in empiricism, that we can gain knowledge from our experience. In Wittgenstein's view, knowledge was limited to logic. When Russell claimed that he knew there was no rhinoceros in the room, Wittgenstein refused to accept this. It was logically possible that there *was* a rhinoceros in the room. Russell then asked him where this rhinoceros could possibly be, and began looking behind the chairs and under the table. Still Wittgenstein adamantly refused to accept that Russell knew for certain there was no rhinoceros in the room.

Fortunately (or perhaps unfortunately for philosophy) Russell quickly realized that his impossibly intense and egotistical new student was more than just an obstinate, pestering bore. But he also realized that his new student needed to

16

learn basic logic. At some inconvenience, Russell used his influence and arranged for Wittgenstein to be tutored by a leading Cambridge logician, W. E. Johnson, a fellow of Kings College. The result was a fiasco. "I found in the first hour that he had nothing to teach me," declared Wittgenstein. Johnson ironically observed, "At our first meeting he was teaching me." This arrogant rudeness and inability to listen were to become an increasingly dominant trait in Wittgenstein's character.

Russell generously characterized this period of getting to know Wittgenstein as "one of the most exciting intellectual adventures of my life." He and Wittgenstein began discussing mathematical logic, which at the time was so complex that only half a dozen people in the world could understand it. Yet according to Russell, within two years Wittgenstein "knew all I had to teach." More than this, Wittgenstein had managed to convince Russell that he would never do any creative philosophy again. It was too difficult for him. Only he, Wittgenstein, could possibly discover the way forward.

Wittgenstein had thus found a substitute father and destroyed him. Fortunately Wittgenstein's intellect was just as powerful as his personality. Indeed, it's almost impossible to separate the two, and both had now found their purpose in life. This was more than just a psychological hatchet job by Wittgenstein. The only thing that could stop him from destroying everything, including himself, was the "truth."

It is no exaggeration to compare Wittgenstein wrestling with the problems of logic to Jacob wrestling with his angel. As soon as Wittgenstein discovered philosophy, it became a matter of life and death for him. Anyone who felt it as less than this he viewed with contempt.

But this period of self-realization led to some rather less exalted discoveries. Wittgenstein realized that he was homosexual. He enjoyed spending his time in intense conversation with lonely, intellectual young men but couldn't bring himself to sully these relationships with sensuality. This element in his nature was almost certainly relieved by rare visits to London, or occasional night pickups in the Prater, the main park in Vienna, when he went home. All this only contributed to his psychological turmoil. Here was demonic genius at its purest, aspiring to the heights yet living in shadow, driven to the point where it was all but out of control. After Wittgenstein's father died ("the most beautiful death I can imagine, falling asleep like a child"), he returned to Cambridge to battle the problems of logic with renewed vigor.

There were moments of comparative bliss. In 1913 Wittgenstein went with his friend, the gifted young mathematician David Pinsent, on a summer holiday to Skjolden, a remote village nearly ninety miles up the Hardangerfjord in Norway. Here the two of them enjoyed themselves like thirteen-year-old schoolboys. But Wittgenstein could be an exacting traveling companion, even for an easygoing, self-effacing character like Pinsent. Each morning Wittgenstein insisted on doing logic for several hours. In Pinsent's words: "When he is working he mutters to himself (in a mixture of German and English) and strides up and down all the while." At other times he might take extreme offense over trifles.

When Pinsent stopped to photograph the scenery, or even spoke to someone else on a train, this would provoke an emotional outburst from Wittgenstein, followed by a long sulk. It is difficult to gauge how much this stemmed from his overriding need to dominate, and how much it was due to lover's jealousy (or other conflicts arising from his unspoken love).

As the holiday progressed, Wittgenstein grew increasingly eccentric and neurotic. He became convinced that he was about to die and kept harping on this to Pinsent, who concluded that "he was mad." By now Wittgenstein was breaking new ground in logic and felt he was close to solving the problems that had prevented Russell from discovering the logical foundation for mathematics. The only trouble was, he now felt sure he would die before he could publish the truth. Wittgenstein wrote to Russell, demanding that they meet "as soon as possible" so that Wittgenstein could tell him where he had gone wrong.

Despite this turmoil, when the two vacationers returned to England Wittgenstein informed

Pinsent that this was the best holiday he had ever had. In the understatement of a true Englishman, Pinsent confided to his diary that Wittgenstein had been "trying at times," but he had enough sense to promise himself that he would never vacation with him again.

Meanwhile Wittgenstein was having a series of urgent meetings with Russell. Wittgenstein was in an excited state, and Russell found it impossible to follow his complex logical arguments. But Russell became even more exasperated when Wittgenstein refused to commit himself to paper until he had brought his ideas to perfection. In the end Russell managed to persuade Wittgenstein to let a stenographer be present at their meetings, so that Wittgenstein's answers to Russell's probing questions could be taken down in shorthand.

These stenographer's notes form the basis of Wittgenstein's first work, "Notes on Logic." In it he makes numerous insightful remarks, some of breathtaking simplicity (such as: "'A' is the same as the letter 'A'"). Russell understood at once what Wittgenstein was trying to establish: in order to overcome the paradoxical difficulties of Russell's classes, things needed to be *shown* in symbolic form rather than *said* (because they simply could not be said, and were in fact unsayable). This was difficult to grasp at the best of times. Indeed, probably only Russell really understood what Wittgenstein was getting at. And it looked like it would remain that way, for, as Russell said, "I told him he ought not simply to *state* what he thinks true, but to give arguments for it, but he said arguments spoil its beauty, and that he would feel as if he was dirtying a flower with muddy hands." Wittgenstein was a perfectionist: either you understood perfectly, completely, and at once what he said, or there was no point in listening to what he said at all.

Yet in this unpublished work Wittgenstein did include certain ideas he had about philosophy. These are remarkable for their originality: no one was thinking like this in 1912. And they also contain the conception of philosophy that he was to retain throughout his life: "In philosophy there are no deductions: *it* is purely descriptive." According to Wittgenstein, philosophy gave no picture of reality, and it neither confirmed nor confuted scientific investigation. "Philosophy consists of logic and metaphysics: logic is its basis." It appeared to have little connection with reality and was more concerned with the study of language. "Distrust of grammar is the first requisite for philosophizing."

Wittgenstein had identified philosophy with logic. Here, in embryo, was much of his later philosophy. It could be said that from now on he devoted his life to elaborating these remarks and their implications. But before embarking upon his new philosophy, Wittgenstein decided that perhaps it was time he studied this intriguing subject. There was no harm in finding out what others had been up to. According to Pinsent, "Wittgenstein has only just started systematic reading [in philosophy] and he expresses the most naive surprise that all the philosophers he once worshiped in ignorance are after all stupid and dishonest and make disgusting mistakes." So much for the opposition.

Wittgenstein now decided to return to Norway and live in isolation for the next two years, "doing logic." Even by Wittgenstein's standards this was somewhat drastic. According to Ray Monk's superb biography of Wittgenstein, Russell thought this idea "wild and lunatic." He tried his best to dissuade Wittgenstein: "I said it would be dark, & he said he hated daylight. I said it would be lonely, & he said he prostituted his mind talking to intelligent people. I said he was mad & and he said God preserve him from sanity. (God certainly will.)"

Pinsent was deeply saddened at their farewell. (Although neither of them had the slightest inkling, this was to be their final parting.) Even Wittgenstein seems to have been peripherally perplexed by his decision but was nonetheless determined to go through with it.

Wittgenstein duly sailed to Norway and soon found just the place he was looking for. This was a hut ninety miles up the Hardangerfjord, which could be reached only by rowboat from the remote village of Skjolden. It is difficult to conceive of any place in Europe farther removed from the sophisticated splendors in which he had been brought up—and this was probably the point.

Wittgenstein now embarked upon a long, cold, dark winter of utter solitude, "doing logic." Not surprisingly, he was soon writing to Russell, "I often think I am going mad." But his letters to Russell also contained evidence of the startling advances he was making in logic. These followed directly from Russell's attempt to discover a logical foundation for mathematics, but went even further—attempting to discover a foundation for logic itself.

Wittgenstein asserted that a logical proposition could be shown to be true or false regardless of its constituent parts. For instance, if we say, "This apple is red or not red," this is a tautology (i.e., it is always true). And it will always be true regardless of whether the apple is red or not. Likewise, if we say, "This apple is neither red nor not red," this is a contradiction (i.e., it will always be false). If we had a method for finding out whether a logical proposition is a tautology or a contradiction, or neither, we would have a rule for determining the truth of all propositions.

This rule, stated as a proposition, would be the basis of all logic.

Wittgenstein would never have returned to civilization for anything so trivial as to protect his sanity. But when he learned that his mother was ailing he felt obliged to travel to Vienna. On his arrival he found that he had inherited a fortune. But he preferred that his life not be encumbered with Wittgenstein money, so he decided to give it away. He started by making donations, anonymously, to a number of Austrian poets. His choice of recipients was revealing: one was Rilke, whose cultivated lyrics expressed an intense spirituality; another was Trakl, who hymned his obsession with guilt and decline in a series of dark enigmatic images.

At the outbreak of World War I, Wittgenstein volunteered for the Austro-Hungarian army. His friend Pinsent enlisted with the British army and thus was on the opposing side. Wittgenstein volunteered not because he particularly believed in the cause of the German powers but because he felt it was his duty. As a Wittgenstein he could easily have become an officer, but he chose to remain in the ranks—an extremely dangerous decision. This was the farcically inefficient army of Hasek's *Good Soldier Svejk*, the army whose eastern commander was to dispatch the immortal telegram: "The situation is hopeless but not desperate." Wittgenstein was sent to fight against the Russians on the eastern front, where the carnage matched that of the trenches on the western front in France. He served on a river gunboat in Galicia, then with an artillery battery. Throughout his service Wittgenstein continued to write down his philosophical ideas in notebooks. He was doing original philosophy, but he also remained constantly on the brink of suicide. Despite these distractions, Wittgenstein was an utterly fearless soldier, and his exemplary bravery won him two medals. (Among the soldiering philosophers, his only rival was Socrates.)

Wittgenstein was a parody of the driven personality. Characteristically he saw no reason to try to alleviate this condition by searching for its cause in his own psychological makeup. On the contrary, if only everyone were true to his nature, he thought, everyone could be like this. Wittgenstein rationalized his condition to himself by claiming that life was "an intellectual problem and a moral duty." The intellectual and moral aspects of his personality had so far remained two distinct entities, each spurring the other on. It was only during the war that they fused.

Under constant intellectual pressure (from himself) and the persistent threat of death (from both the enemy and himself), Wittgenstein once again found himself in familiar territory, on the brink of insanity. One day, during a lull in the fighting in Galicia, he came across a bookshop. Here he found Tolstoy's *Gospels in Brief*, which he bought for the simple reason that there was no other book in the shop. Wittgenstein had been against Christianity—he associated it with Vienna, his family, lack of a logical foundation, meek and mild behavior, and other anathemas. But reading through Tolstoy's book was to bring the light of religion into Wittgenstein's life. Within days he had become a convinced Christian—though his conversion had a distinctly

28

Wittgensteinian tenor. With typical rigor he set about integrating his beliefs into his intellectual life.

Religious remarks now began appearing in the pages of his notebooks, alongside those on logic. And it soon becomes clear that these two topics have more than intellectual rigor in common. The spirit of one informs the other in compelling fashion. Even Wittgenstein's religion had to assume a logical force and clarity: "I know that this world exists. That I am placed in it like an eye in its visual field." There was something problematic about the world, and this we called its meaning. But this meaning did not lie within the world, it lay outside it. "The meaning of life, i.e., the meaning of the world, we can call God." According to Wittgenstein, to pray was to think about the meaning of life. (Which meant that he had been praying all his life, even when he didn't believe there was a God or a meaning to life. Wittgenstein couldn't bear to be wrong—ever.)

Wittgenstein then passes on to the question of the will—an overriding element in his life, if not in his philosophy. He opens with the uncontroversial assertion that he knows his will penetrates the world. He then passes on to claim that he knows "my will is good or evil. Therefore good and evil are somehow connected with the meaning of the world." But how does Wittgenstein "know" that his will is good or evil—and what precisely does he mean by these two terms? Also, if his will is within the world, and the meaning of the world lies outside it, it is difficult to see how they can be "somehow connected."

Once again Wittgenstein seemed to consider that argument only spoiled the beauty of his striking assertions. Russell had tried to correct this bad philosophic habit, but by now he was locked away in a British prison for demonstrating against the war. Wittgenstein was to persist in this infuriating practice, which flawed his early philosophical work. But was it a drawback? Wittgenstein appeared to have an inkling of what he was up to. Making such striking assertions, but leaving them devoid of blurring justification or argument, gave what he said an almost oracular force. Could Wittgenstein have been more concerned with effect than with truth? He would have been horrified by such a suggestion. Yet there's no denying this thin but distinct thread of what looks suspiciously like showmanship, which runs through his life and work. Like it or not, his was a personality of mythical proportions (and for the most part he genuinely disliked this). One can only assume that his attraction to the limelight was at least partly subconscious.

In 1918 Wittgenstein was promoted to officer and transferred to the Italian front. Somehow he had managed to correspond intermittently with his friend David Pinsent throughout the war, but he now received news that Pinsent had been killed. "I want to tell you how much he loved you up to the last," wrote Pinsent's mother, oblivious to the irony of her remark. (All the evidence indicates that Pinsent remained unaware of the true nature of Wittgenstein's feelings for him.) Wittgenstein wrote back to her that David was "my first and my only friend." He was to dedicate his first great work to David Pinsent's memory.

In 1918 the Austro-Hungarian war effort

came to an end in ignoble surrender. In Italy many of the Austrian officers simply boarded a train back to Austria, abandoning their men to their fate. But not Lieutenant Wittgenstein, who would have been incapable of such an act. (It is almost impossible to exaggerate how much Wittgenstein's life was driven by principle. His moments of greatest despair always came when he temporarily relaxed and was able to see how far below his impossibly high principles his life was falling.)

When Wittgenstein was taken prisoner by the Italians, he had in his rucksack the only manuscript of the philosophical work he had been writing throughout the war. This was eventually to be called *Tractatus Logico-Philosophicus*, and is the first great philosophical work of the modern era. Right from its opening sentences it becomes obvious that philosophy has entered a new stage.

"1   The world is all that is the case.

"1.1   The world is the totality of facts, not of things."

One clear, ringing assertion follows another,

linked by the absolute minimum of justification or argument:

"1.13   The facts in logical space are the world.

"1.2   The world divides into facts."

The book's conclusion is even more memorable:

"7   What we cannot speak about we must pass over in silence."

Few others have altered the course of philosophy in quite so striking a fashion. Such succinct perspicacity is surpassed only by Socrates ("Know thyself"), Descartes ("I think, therefore I am"), and Nietzsche ("God is dead"). In those parts where it is not too technical (in the logical sense), Wittgenstein's *Tractatus* is the most exciting work of philosophy ever written. Its clarity and daring leaps of argument make it at times almost poetic, as do many of its conclusions. And its basic idea is simple to grasp.

The *Tractatus* is an attempt to delineate what we can talk about in a meaningful manner. This leads to the question, What is language? Wittgenstein claims that language gives us a picture of the world. This idea had been inspired by a newspaper report he had read about a court case in which model cars had been used to represent an accident. The model cars were like language describing the actual state of affairs. They pictured what had happened, but most important they shared the same "logical form"—they both obeyed the rules of logic. The model cars (language) could also be used to describe all possibilities (near miss, traffic jam, absence of car that was alleged to have caused the accident, and so forth). But they could not describe two cars occupying the same space at once, or one car occupying two separate spaces at once. Logical form prevented this—both in reality and in language.

When it is analyzed down to its atomic propositions, language consists of pictures of reality. In this way propositions can represent the whole of reality, all facts—because propositions and reality have the same logical form. They *cannot* be illogical.

The limits of language are the limits of thought, because this too cannot be illogical. We cannot go beyond language, for to do so would be to go beyond the limits of logical possibility. The logical propositions of language are a picture of the world and can be nothing else. They can say nothing about anything else. This means that certain things simply cannot be said. Unfortunately the assertions in the *Tractatus* fall into this category. These assertions are not pictures of the world.

Wittgenstein realized this. In trying to overcome this difficulty, he clung to his earlier idea that although certain things cannot be *said* to be true, they can be *shown* to be true. He admitted that in the *Tractatus* he was trying to say what can in fact only be shown. But he concludes the *Tractatus* with his celebrated magisterial pronouncement which forbids others from trying the same: "What we cannot speak about we must pass over in silence."

Inevitably God falls into this category of things that cannot be spoken about. We can't say anything about God because language pictures only reality. Yet Wittgenstein claims that such things as God do exist, it's just that they can't be said or thought. "There are, indeed, things that cannot be put into words. They *make themselves manifest*. They are what is mystical." In common with his writings in his wartime notebooks, the end of the *Tractatus* is a compelling blend of logic and mysticism. It is very difficult to dismiss this as hocus-pocus, especially when it is expressed with such forceful clarity. Unfortunately it is not philosophy, though it probably qualifies as philosophic poetry of the highest order.

Sadly there are a number of even more crucial objections to the *Tractatus*. Admittedly language and reality certainly have some relation to each other. But how do we know that this relation is in fact "logical form"? Wittgenstein was forced to fudge this issue (though he certainly didn't believe this was what he was doing). Also, the category of things we cannot talk about includes a large number of things that we simply must talk about if we are to continue living in a civilized fashion. For a start, we can't talk about good and evil (or even right and wrong). Likewise, the "language" of art also falls into this category, for it is in essence illogical. In being metaphorical, a work of art is both itself and something else. And to say of a work of art that what it expresses is inexpressible is a contradiction. (Even Wittgenstein would find it difficult to argue that it doesn't express anything at all.) Some have argued that language itself falls into this category. Wittgenstein overcomes this problem by declaring that since logical propositions are tautologous they do in fact "say nothing." This admission would appear to put an end to philosophy as such. Wittgenstein has the good grace (or overweening pride) to point this out in his preface to the *Tractatus*.

Despite these serious objections and the admission of philosophic bankruptcy, the *Tractatus* was to have a profound influence. In particular, it proved an inspiration to the Vienna Circle, who formulated Logical Positivism. Philosophy may have come to an end, but it didn't stop the Logical Positivists from developing this end into a further philosophy of their own. According to them, the meaning of any proposition lies in its manner of verification. There are two meaningful types of propositions. In the first, which are to be found in mathematics and logic, the meaning of the subject is contained in the meaning of the predicate. They are tautologous, and this can be verified by comparing the subject with the predicate—for example, "Twelve minus ten is two." The second type of proposition is verifiable by observation—for example, "The ball is rolling down the hill." If you can't verify a statement, it is meaningless. This rules out all metaphysics, which includes theological statements such as "God exists." According to Wittgenstein, such a question as "Does God exist?" is not only incapable of being answered but incapable of being asked in the first place, as it is meaningless. We simply cannot speak in any meaningful fashion about what isn't tautologous or verifiable by observation. Yet, unlike the Logical Positivists, Wittgenstein continued to believe in God—even if it was impossible to speak about him.

Wittgenstein's concluding remark—"What we cannot speak about we must pass over in silence"—also presents a problem. If it is impossible to speak about a thing in a meaningful manner, we must keep quiet about it. God, ethics, aesthetics, identifying the winner of the Kentucky Derby before the race—are all consigned to silence. Unfortunately, such statements as "What we cannot speak about we must pass over in silence" also fall into the same category, but Wittgenstein didn't consider this to be a fatal flaw in his argument.

Wittgenstein put the finishing touches to the *Tractatus Logico-Philosophicus* while being held under conditions of extreme privation in an Italian prisoner-of-war camp at Cassino. From here he managed to make contact with Russell, and eventually the *Tractatus* was published with a preface by Russell. This preface outraged and disillusioned Wittgenstein, because he considered that it showed Russell hadn't understood his book. Wittgenstein insisted upon including his own introduction as a corrective. In this he modestly points out that his work contains "the unassailable and definitive . . . truth . . . the final solution of the problems [of philosophy]." He does have the good grace to admit "how little is achieved when these problems are solved."

Having put an end to philosophy, Wittgenstein quite logically saw no point in continuing with this subject. When he returned home to Austria after the war, he began looking around for another field of endeavor. He thought of entering a monastery but considered the monk who greeted him at the gate offensively rude, so he abandoned the idea and took up working as a gardener on the monastery grounds. He was determined to lead the life of a saint (even if his philosophy had denied the meaningful existence of saints, rendering them unspeakable). In fact, Wittgenstein was once again a deeply troubled man. In the extremes of war he had undergone a form of religious conversion and now believed in living a simple spiritual life, similar to that preached by Tolstoy during his last years.

The Austro-Hungarian Empire was in ruins, and Austria itself was bankrupt both spiritually and financially. But on the instructions of Karl Wittgenstein before he died, the family fortune had been reinvested in America. To his son Ludwig's irritation, this meant that he was now even richer than he had been before the war, when he

40

had tried to give away his inheritance. In between hoeing the monastery garden, Wittgenstein visited Vienna to make sure that this time the family lawyer followed his instructions to the letter and gave away all his inherited fortune. This took some time, as the lawyer at first found his instructions impossible to believe, and then was astonished by how much he was expected to get rid of. Eventually he managed to pass on most of it to Wittgenstein's sisters, who had no wish to see more of the family fortune frittered away on donations to otherworldly or alcoholic poets.

Having got rid of philosophy and his inherited millions, Wittgenstein decided to become a schoolteacher in a remote mountain village in lower Austria. After turning down one village because it had a pleasant little park with a fountain ("This is not for me, I want an entirely rural spot"), he happened upon the poor village of Trattenbach.

Wittgenstein's sojourn here was a catastrophe for all concerned. The aristocratic saint began inflicting his impossible principles upon the peasant children, whose parents were outraged. (They needed no teaching about poverty and simplicity.) The God-fearing villagers were equally outraged when the resident saint refused to attend church because he thought the sermons spiritually vacuous. And they were even more put out when he refused to join them for a drink in the local *bierstube*, instead choosing to remain upstairs in his bare room playing the clarinet (and contemplating suicide). After a couple of years things came to a head. In an incident at the school, Wittgenstein struck a child. This was blown up out of all proportion, and the villagers managed to rid themselves of their philosophically impossible saint.

Wittgenstein returned to Vienna, where his family became seriously worried about his mental condition. One of his sisters commissioned him to build a new house for her, and he took on the task with characteristic earnestness, designing a modern blocklike building utterly devoid of ornamentation. But this was to be no simple construction; each element of the design had to be fulfilled with fanatical exactitude. An entire

42

wall was knocked down when a window was found to be a few centimeters out of place; each doorhandle had to be specially made; the window latches were discovered to be aesthetically unacceptable; and so on. The builders were driven to distraction by their perfectionist taskmaster. But they couldn't afford to leave the employ of this lunatic who was building his millionairess sister a three-story modern residential prison, because out on the streets of Vienna people were starving.

This house still stands on Kundmangasse, a street close to the Danube canal in an eastern district of Vienna. In appearance the building is a rather unexceptional, early-twentieth-century modernist block, three stories high, with rows of large plain windows. When I first located the Wittgensteinhaus several years ago, I was informed that it was not open to the public. Disappointedly I stood in the street, trying to peer up through the windows in an attempt to see what it looked like inside. Through one of the windows I noticed a staircase, which crossed it diagonally. After a few moments I quickly turned away. A woman had begun ascending the stair-case, and I found myself gazing up under her skirt. This structural howler had evidently been overlooked by the architect amidst his obsession with precisely positioned and impeccably de-signed light switches and the like. (In a striking parallel, Wittgenstein's second philosophy, which must have been forming in his mind at the time, shows remarkably similar characteristics in its obsession with detail and complete disregard for the requirements of the people who are ex-pected to live with it.)

At the same time Wittgenstein was building this house for his sister, he regularly met with members of the Vienna Circle. This discussion group contained some of the finest minds in cen-tral Europe, including the philosopher Schlick (who was later shot by a student disappointed with his exam results) and the logician Carnap (who came to believe that all philosophical prob-lems would be solved if we would all speak Es-peranto).

The members of the Vienna Circle were in the process of developing the ideas in Wittgenstein's *Tractatus* into the virulent antimeta-physics of Logical Positivism. They were as-tounded to find that Wittgenstein himself was a deeply spiritual man. They should have been warned: the *Tractatus* has a prevalent strain of cryptic mysticism. ("It is not how things are in the world that is mystical, but that it exists.") By way of an explanation, Wittgenstein claimed that what he had not said in the *Tractatus* was much more important than what he had said. The best minds in central Europe listened in baf-fled silence as the modern saint, who couldn't exist, attempted to explain what he hadn't said, which couldn't be said. This philosophical In-dian rope trick led Wittgenstein to realize that perhaps he hadn't quite succeeded in killing off philosophy after all.

This was a unique event. Never before had a major philosopher admitted, even to himself, that his philosophy was wrong. But Wittgenstein characteristically went one step further. Since his philosophy was wrong, *all* philosophy was obvi-ously wrong. He now embarked on his second attempt to destroy philosophy once and for all.

In 1929 he returned to Cambridge. The only philosopher in the world who could possibly have understood what he was talking about was Russell, and it quickly became clear to Russell that he had no idea what Wittgenstein was talking about. The faculty decided to admit Wittgenstein as a fellow of Trinity College all the same (despite the fact that he hadn't even taken a degree).

Wittgenstein lectured at Cambridge for the next eighteen years, all the while typically belaboring himself for doing something so "dishonest," and describing philosophy as "a kind of living death." In his lectures he began elaborating his new philosophy, or antiphilosophy. These are the legendary lectures that were held in Wittgenstein's ascetically bare rooms, which can still be seen in Whewell's Court at Trinity College, overlooking a quiet little courtyard with a lawn and a bronze statue of a naked youth. The only ornament in Wittgenstein's rooms was a safe, where he kept the papers containing the philosophy that no one else could understand. The chosen few who were permitted to attend

Wittgenstein's lectures were required to bring their own deck chairs. They would sit in silence while Wittgenstein held his head, "thinking." Occasionally, with every appearance of extreme effort, the philosopher would deliver himself of a "thought." With anyone else but Wittgenstein this would have been a farcically pretentious demonstration of "original thinking." But all who were present agree that the atmosphere was electric. Occasionally Wittgenstein would grill one of his "students," who included some of the best brains in Cambridge, the usual lonely intellectual young men, and in later years a black U.S. air force man who wandered in uninvited one day and was asked to stay because of his "cheery face." (Meanwhile, professors from Cornell and elsewhere who had crossed the Atlantic to hear Wittgenstein frequently were refused admittance.)

All are agreed that when Wittgenstein interrogated one of his students on a philosophical point, the nearest equivalent was the Spanish Inquisition. Wittgenstein had a personality of such domineering force that he reduced his audience to a state of terror. The only man who was known to have stood up to him was Turing, inventor of the computer and one of the finest mathematicians of the age (who was later forced to abandon his mathematical career to help win World War II by cracking the Germans' Enigma code). During one of Wittgenstein's lectures he suggested that a system such as logic or mathematics could remain valid even if it contained a contradiction. Turing disagreed: there was no point in building a bridge with mathematics that contained a hidden contradiction, or the bridge might fall down. Wittgenstein refused to accept this: empirical considerations played no part in logic. But Turing refused to be browbeaten and went on insisting that the bridge would fall down. (The parallel with the application of Wittgenstein's philosophy to real life provides interesting food for thought.)

During his time at Cambridge, Wittgenstein became something of a *monstre sacre* for the university. He would turn up at the weekly meetings of the Philosophical Club and monopolize the discussions, aggressively destroying the arguments of professors and undergraduates alike. He remained intensely lonely but managed to form a few relationships with his lonely intellectual young men, one of whom he ended up living with. Invariably he dominated these relationships, which were for the most part platonic, but he often caused great harm to his companions. He would insist that they give up their academic pursuits and live a life of Tolstoyan simplicity, working in a local factory or becoming a hospital porter.

At the outbreak of World War II Wittgenstein too became a hospital porter. Fortunately his highly placed friends at the university had managed to secure for him British nationality, but he suffered deeply over the fact that he was safe while his sisters remained in Nazi-occupied Vienna. The Wittgensteins were Jewish, and despite being the Austrian equivalent of the Rothschilds, their safety was far from assured. (Ludwig was not the only one to inherit the Wittgenstein trait of principled arrogance. When a Nazi official informed his sister that the Wittgensteins need have no fear they would be classified as Jews, she was highly indignant. No mere upstart was about to tell the Wittgensteins what they were or were not, and she insisted upon papers certifying that she was of Jewish blood.)

In 1944 Wittgenstein returned to Cambridge and began preparing for publication a manuscript containing his new philosophy. This was to be called *Philosophical Investigations* and was finally published in 1953. This, and the *Tractatus*, which he now disowned, were to be the only two books that Wittgenstein prepared for publication during his lifetime. More than half a dozen works appeared posthumously; these were made up of lecture notes taken by his "students," and several notebooks from the famous safe.

Some have found it symbolic that this safe was the only luxury that Wittgenstein permitted himself during his long ascetic period. The man who longed for clarity in both his life and work kept many dark secrets locked within him. Similarly, others have commented on the resemblance between his pronouncement "What we cannot speak about we must pass over in silence" and his attitude toward his homosexuality. A life so intense as Wittgenstein's is bound to be rich in such parallels. But here we are perhaps better off following another of his famous remarks: Little that is meaningful can be said about such matters, they can only be shown.

In comparison to the *Tractatus*, Wittgenstein's *Philosophical Investigations* is a bitter disappointment. The lucid clarity and daring of the *Tractatus* is replaced by nit-picking logical analysis of particular sensations and the meaning of words. There is no such thing as philosophy any more, just philosophizing, which consists of unraveling mistakes in our thinking. These arise through linguistic errors. Language is not a picture of the world, it is like a net that consists of many pieces of interconnected string. Our understanding becomes knotted when we misuse a word in a situation to which it does not apply. The duty of philosophy is painstakingly to unravel these knots. This is why philosophy is now so complex (and so boring). The long and glorious tradition of philosophy, and its profound questions which formed an integral part of our culture, are now reduced to linguistic rummaging. Wittgenstein's later philosophy has recently been compared to the Superstring Theory in science, which states that the fundamental sub-atomic particles that make up the universe are like pieces of interlocking string. This comparison is false—only one of these cat's-cradle theories could possibly prove interesting.

Having created his second philosophy, Wittgenstein went off once again to become a saint. He lived for a while in a remote cottage in the west of Ireland, where he did his thinking and fed the seagulls. But he soon became too ill to live such an austere life, and began staying with various friends in England and America. Eventually cancer was diagnosed, and he died in Cambridge on April 29, 1951. Although never a churchgoing Christian, he had requested a Catholic burial. His grave, with its suitably plain tombstone giving simply his name and dates, can be seen in the grassy, pleasantly unkempt graveyard of St. Giles's Church (which is a mile up the Huntingdon Road from the church itself). When

I visited this spot, on a cold, misty February afternoon, the borders of Wittgenstein's grave had been planted by an admirer with little winter-flowering pansies (which almost certainly would not have met with the aesthetic approval of its occupant). The gravestone itself was slightly scuffed, suggesting the rather clumsy (or possibly disrespectful) attentions of undergraduates. To this day the notorious philosophicide continues to attract his uncalled-for devotees.

Afterword

Wittgenstein outlined his legacy in the unpublished foreword to his *Philosophical Remarks.* There he explains that his philosophy is intended only for those who are in sympathy with the spirit in which it was written. As Russell observed, Wittgenstein had the pride of Lucifer— but he also possessed the spiritual fanaticism of a saint. "What is good is also divine. Queer as it sounds, that sums up my ethics. Only something supernatural can express the Supernatural." He was determined he would live his life on this level, or not at all. (The continual question of suicide was not merely a psychological inheritance, it was a moral problem.)

Wittgenstein was aware that this attitude was not in "the spirit of the main current of European and American civilization." Although he may have been the greatest philosopher of the twentieth century, he spent his entire life in conflict with it. He found "the industry, architecture and music of our time, in its fascism and socialism . . . alien and uncongenial." Characteristically he insisted, "This is not a value judgment." In such matters he evidently considered himself to be above matters of mere human taste, or even of history. Despite this he went on to make what look curiously like value judgments about many aspects of modern culture. He refused to accept "what nowadays passes for architecture as architecture" (his own effort in this field is passed over in silence). He viewed "what is called modern music with the greatest suspicion (though without understanding its language)." This confession does not appear to be one of modesty but rather an indication that he considers himself above such matters. And it certainly doesn't prevent him from passing more sweeping judgments, where arrogance is tempered with apparent compassion. "The disappearance of the arts does not justify judging disparagingly the human beings who make up this civilization." In times like this, "genuine strong characters" abandon the arts and turn to other things—such as putting an end to philosophy, perhaps. We are presented with "the unimpressive spectacle of a crowd whose best members work for purely private ends." In an age that saw the rise of popular democracy and the liberation of vast numbers of downtrodden humanity, he observed, "I have no sympathy for the current of European civilization and do not understand its goals, if it has any." But he did concede that "the disappearance of a culture does not signify the disappearance of human value, but simply of certain means of expressing this value." Having dispensed with the cultural expression of human values, Wittgenstein introduced a philosophy that insisted we must remain silent about such matters. He left humanity gagged.

Despite his protests to the contrary, Wittgenstein was curiously in accord with the spirit of his age. During his time human values were largely determined by those who had no use for philosophy—the populists and demagogues who shaped the public ethos of the twentieth century. In the private realm, be it called spiritual or personal, things remain more problematic.

As a consequence of Wittgenstein's philosophy, the questions once asked by philosophy have now passed into the realms of poetry. The way poetry is going, it looks as if they won't be asked much longer here either. We have learned to do without God, and it looks as if we will learn to do without philosophy. It will now, alas, join the ranks of subjects which are completed (and have become completely spurious), such as alchemy, astrology, platonic love, and stylitism.

From Wittgenstein's Writings

Wittgenstein opens his Tractatus Logico-Philosophicus *with two striking remarks:*

1   The world is all that is the case.

1.1   The world is the totality of facts, not of things.

He then argues:

1.12   For the totality of facts determines what is the case, and also whatever is not the case.

1.13   The facts in logical space are the world.

This leads on to:

2 What is the case—a fact—is the existence of states of affairs.

2.01 A state of affairs (a state of things) is a combination of objects (things).

He then claims:

2.012 In logic nothing is accidental: if a thing *can* occur in a state of affairs, the possibility of the state of affairs must be written into the thing itself.

Later he states his ethical position:

6.421 It is clear that ethics cannot be put into words. Ethics is transcendental. (Ethics and aesthetics are one and the same.)

6.43 If the good or bad exercise of the will does alter the world, it can alter only the limits of the world, not the facts—not what can be expressed by means of language.

He reveals that his attitude is essentially mystical:

6.432   *How* things are in the world is a matter of complete indifference to what is higher. God does not reveal himself *in* the facts.

This leads him to denigrate philosophy:

6.53   The correct method in philosophy would really be the following: to say nothing except what can be said, i.e., propositions of natural science—i.e., something that has nothing to do with philosophy—and then, whenever someone else wanted to say something metaphysical to demonstrate to him that he had failed to give a meaning to certain signs in his propositions.

He then modestly denigrates his own philosophy:

6.54   My propositions serve as elucidations in the following way: anyone who understands me eventually recognizes them as nonsensical, when he has used them—as steps—to climb up beyond them. (He must, so to speak, throw away the ladder after he has climbed up it.)

This leads to his final, controversial conclusion:

7   What we cannot speak about we must pass over in silence.

> —*Tractatus Logico-Philosophicus*
> (trans. Pears and McGuiness)

In his later work, Philosophical Investigations, *Wittgenstein reduces his philosophy to linguistic analysis:*

30.   So one might say: the ostensive definition explains the use—the meaning—of the word when the overall role of the word in language is clear.

He gives an example:

Thus if I know that someone means to explain a color-word to me, the ostensive definition "That is called 'sepia'" will help me to understand the word.—And you can say this so long as you do not forget that all sorts of problems attach to the words "to know" or "to be clear."

He elaborates with a further example:

31.   When one shows someone the king in chess and says: "This is the king," this does not tell him the use of the piece—unless he already knows the rules of the game up to this last point: the shape of the king. You could imagine him

having learned the rules of the game without ever having been shown an actual piece. The shape of the chessman corresponds here to the sound or shape of the word.

This eventually leads him to the conclusion:

123.   A philosophical problem has the form: "I don't know my way about."

But he warns:

124.   Philosophy may in no way interfere with the actual use of language; it can in the end only describe it.
   For it cannot give it any foundation either.
   It leaves everything as it is. . . .

As a result the scope of philosophy is reduced:

125.   It is the business of philosophy not to re-

solve a contradiction by means of a mathematical or logic-mathematical discovery, but to make it possible for us to get a clear view of the state of ... affairs *before* the contradiction is resolved. (And this does not mean that one is sidestepping a difficulty.)

This leads to a tangled situation from which it appears almost impossible to escape:

The fundamental fact here is that we lay down rules, a technique, for a game, and that when we then follow the rules, things do not turn out as we had assumed. That we are therefore, as it were, entangled in our own rules.

The entanglement in our rules is what we want to understand (i.e., get a clear view of).

—*Philosophical Investigations*
(trans. G. E. M. Anscombe)

Wittgenstein insisted upon logic, and in doing so imposed severe limits upon philosophical think-

ing. Indeed, many have come to see this as a stranglehold which prevents us from thinking about matters that have been the traditional concerns of philosophy. In light of this, it is instructive to see how logic was viewed in the previous century by Nietzsche:

Suppose there was no self-identical "A," such as is assumed by every proposition of logic (and mathematics), and this "A" was already a mere appearance—in this case logic would merely be about a world of appearances. In fact, we believe in this proposition merely because our experience seems always to confirm it. The "thing"— this is what really underlies "A." *Our belief in things*: this is the precondition of our belief in logic. . . .

Our very first acts of thought—affirmation and denial, decisions about truth and untruth— are . . . already influenced by our belief that we can discover true knowledge, that our judgments can be the truth. . . .

This is the origin of our basic sensualistic

prejudice that sensations tell us the truth about the world—that I cannot simultaneously maintain that a thing is hard and that it is also soft. . . .

The conceptual ban on contradiction stems from our belief that we *can* form concepts, that these concepts not only specify the essence of a thing but also *understand* it. In fact, logic (just like geometry and arithmetic) applies only to fictions of our own creation. Logic is our attempt to understand the actual world by using a scheme which we ourselves have made up. In other words, to make it amenable to schemes of formula and calculation which we have invented for ourselves alone.

—*Will to Power*, Sec 516

In Culture and Value, *Wittgenstein reflects on a wider range of topics beyond the realms of logic and logical philosophy. Here he reveals many of the traits that made him such a difficult customer in everyday life:*

The reason why I cannot understand Shakespeare is that I want to find symmetry in all this asymmetry.

His pieces give an impression as of enormous *sketches* rather than of paintings; as though they had been *dashed off* by someone who can permit himself *anything*. . . . Anyone who admires them as one admires, say, Beethoven, seems to me to misunderstand Shakespeare.

The arrogance of this remark speaks for itself. And how anyone who doesn't understand Shakespeare (and so aptly demonstrates this) can claim that those who do *understand Shakespeare misunderstand him, can be clear only to a master logician. Alas Wittgenstein never encountered the schoolmaster who once said to me, "I'd like to hear your opinion on this piece of Beethoven. And remember, it is not Beethoven who is being examined here."*

When judging another great artist, Wittgenstein reveals a trait that constantly recurred in his dealings with others:

If it is true that Mahler's music is worthless, as I believe to be the case, then the question is what I think he ought to have done with his talent. . . . Should he, say, have written his symphonies and then burned them? Or should he have done violence to himself and not written them? Should he have written them and realized that they were worthless? But how could he have realized that? I can see it, because I can compare his music with what the great composers wrote. But *he* could not, because . . . his nature is not that of other great composers.

—*Culture and Value* (trans. Peter Winch)

Such remarks would be laughable if Wittgenstein had not put them into practice. He had a nasty habit of interfering drastically in the lives of those around him. He browbeat his friend Skinner into abandoning a brilliant academic career and becoming a factory hand. Someone who sought advice about becoming a surgeon in the Royal Army Medical Corps was told he should volunteer for the front as a private. While at

Cambridge, Wittgenstein also spent considerable effort trying to persuade the leading literary critic F. R. Leavis that he was not suited to the study of English literature and should give it up. This from the man who admitted that he didn't understand Shakespeare.

Chronology of Significant Philosophical Dates

6th C B.C.   The beginning of Western philosophy
                 with Thales of Miletus.

End of
6th C B.C.   Death of Pythagoras.

399 B.C.   Socrates sentenced to death in
                 Athens.

c 387 B.C.   Plato founds the Academy in Athens,
                 the first university.

335 B.C.   Aristotle founds the Lyceum in
                 Athens, a rival school to the
                 Academy.

324 A.D.	Emperor Constantine moves capital of Roman Empire to Byzantium.
400 A.D.	St. Augustine writes his *Confessions*. Philosophy absorbed into Christian theology.
410 A.D.	Sack of Rome by Visigoths heralds opening of Dark Ages.
529 A.D.	Closure of Academy in Athens by Emperor Justinian marks end of Hellenic thought.
Mid-13th C	Thomas Aquinas writes his commentaries on Aristotle. Era of Scholasticism.
1453	Fall of Byzantium to Turks, end of Byzantine Empire.
1492	Columbus reaches America. Renaissance in Florence and revival of interest in Greek learning.
1543	Copernicus publishes *On the Revolution of the Celestial Orbs*, proving mathematically that the earth revolves around the sun.

1633	Galileo forced by church to recant heliocentric theory of the universe.
1641	Descartes publishes his *Meditations*, the start of modern philosophy.
1677	Death of Spinoza allows publication of his *Ethics*.
1687	Newton publishes *Principia*, introducing concept of gravity.
1689	Locke publishes *Essay Concerning Human Understanding*. Start of empiricism.
1710	Berkeley publishes *Principles of Human Knowledge*, advancing empiricism to new extremes.
1716	Death of Leibniz.
1739–1740	Hume publishes *Treatise of Human Nature*, taking empiricism to its logical limits.
1781	Kant, awakened from his "dogmatic slumbers" by Hume, publishes *Critique of Pure Reason*.

Great era of German metaphysics begins.

1807 Hegel publishes *The Phenomenology of Mind*, high point of German metaphysics.

1818 Schopenhauer publishes *The World as Will and Representation*, introducing Indian philosophy into German metaphysics.

1889 Nietzsche, having declared "God is dead," succumbs to madness in Turin.

1921 Wittgenstein publishes *Tractatus Logico-Philosophicus*, claiming the "final solution" to the problems of philosophy.

1920s Vienna Circle propounds Logical Positivism.

1927 Heidegger publishes *Being and Time*, heralding split between analytical and Continental philosophy.

1943 Sartre publishes *Being and Nothingness*, advancing

Heidegger's thought and instigating existentialism.

1953   Posthumous publication of Wittgenstein's *Philosophical Investigations*. High era of linguistic analysis.

Chronology of
Wittgenstein's Life

1889	Ludwig Wittgenstein born in Vienna, April 26.
1906	Goes to Berlin to study engineering.
1908	Registers as research student at Manchester University, England.
1912	Admitted to Trinity College, Cambridge, to study logic with Bertrand Russell.
1914	Volunteers for Austro-Hungarian army upon outbreak of World War I.

1918	Taken prisoner-of-war in Italy.
1920	Becomes schoolteacher in remote Austrian village of Trattenbach.
1921	First publication of *Tractatus Logico-Philosophicus* in *Annalen der Naturphilosophie* (first appears in book form with English translation a year later).
1927	Discusses philosophy with Vienna Circle in Vienna.
1929	Returns to Cambridge.
1930	Becomes fellow of Trinity College.
1939	Elected professor of philosophy at Cambridge.
1940	Works as a porter at a London hospital.
1947	Resigns chair at Cambridge and moves to remote cottage in Ireland.
1951	Dies at the age of sixty-two of cancer in Cambridge.

Chronology of Wittgenstein's Era

1889	Erection of Eiffel Tower in Paris.
1900	Death of Nietzsche. Freud publishes *The Interpretation of Dreams*.
1903	Curies awarded Nobel Prize for discovery of radioactivity.
1905	Einstein publishes "Special Theory of Relativity."
1912	Sinking of the *Titanic*.
1913	Bohr proposes Quantum Theory.
1914–1918	World War I.

1917	Bolshevik Revolution in Russia.
1919	Disintegration of Austro-Hungarian Empire.
1922	Schlick founds Vienna Circle. Publication of Joyce's *Ulysses* and Eliot's "The Waste Land."
1927	Heidegger publishes *Being and Time*.
1929	Wall Street crash heralds era of the Great Depression.
1939–1945	World War II.
1945	Explosion of first atomic bomb. Founding of United Nations. Era of existentialism in Paris.
1948–1949	Berlin airlift.
1950	Outbreak of Korean War.

Recommended Reading

A. Phillips Griffiths, ed., *Wittgenstein: Centenary Essays* (Cambridge University Press, 1991)

Anthony Kenny, ed., *The Wittgenstein Reader* (Blackwell, 1994)

Ray Monk, *Ludwig Wittgenstein: The Duty of Genius* (Viking Penguin, 1991)

David Pears, *The False Prison: A Study of the Development of Wittgenstein's Philosophy* (Oxford University Press, 1987–1988)

Joachim Schulte, *Experience and Expression: Wittgenstein's Philosophy of Psychology* (Oxford University Press, 1993)

81

Index

A NOTE ON THE AUTHOR

Paul Strathern has lectured in philosophy and mathematics and now lives and writes in London. A Somerset Maugham prize winner, he is also the author of books on history and travel as well as five novels. His articles have appeared in a great many publications, including the *Observer* (London) and the *Irish Times*. His own degree in philosophy was earned at Trinity College, Dublin.